WATER FOR EVERYONE

Sally Morgan

SEA-TO-SEA

Mankato Collingwood London

This edition first published in 2010 by
Sea-to-Sea Publications
Distributed by Black Rabbit Books
P.O. Box 3263, Mankato, Minnesota 56002

Printed in USA

Library of Congress Cataloging-in-Publication Data

Morgan, Sally.
  Water for everyone / Sally Morgan.
      p. cm. -- (Earth SOS)
  Includes index.
  ISBN 978-1-59771-227-9 (hardcover)
  1. Water-supply--Juvenile literature. I. Title.
  TD348.M68 2010
  363.6'1--dc22
                                  2008053173

9 8 7 6 5 4 3 2

Published by arrangement with the Watts
Publishing Group Ltd., London

EARTH SOS is based on the series *EarthWatch* published by Franklin Watts.
It was produced for Franklin Watts by Bender Richardson White,
P O Box 266, Uxbridge UB9 5NX.
Project Editor: Lionel Bender
Text Editor: Jenny Vaughan
Original text adapted and updated by: Jenny Vaughan
Designer: Ben White
Picture Researchers: Cathy Stastny and Daniela Marceddu
Media Conversion and Make-up: Mike Weintroub, MW Graphics,
and Clare Oliver
Production: Kim Richardson

Picture Credits: Panos Pictures: cover top photo (Liba Taylor) and pages
5 (Giacomo Pirozzi), 6 (Chris Sattleberger), 10 (Howard Davies), 11
bottom (Cliff Venner), 15 bottom (Liba Taylor), 23 top, 25 bottom and
29 bottom (Jeremy Hartley). Oxford Scientific Films: pages 7 (Richard
Packwood), 9 bottom (Doug Allan). Lionel Bender: cover main photo.
Ecoscene: pages 1 and 20 (Blowfield), 26–27 (Andrew Brown).
Environmental Images: pages 15 top (Vanessa Miles), 21 top (Colin
Cumming). Science Photo Library, London: pages 4 left (ESA/Photo
Library International), 4–5 (David Frazier/Agstock), 14 and 17 (Martin
Bond). Still Pictures: pages 8 (Mark Edwards), 18–19 (David Drain), 22
(Hartmut Schwarzbach). Tony Stone Images: pages 9 top (Mike Severns),
13 (Penny Tweedie), 16 (Greg Pease), 19 (Arnulf Husmo), 21 bottom
(Mark Wagner), 26 (Jonathan Morgan), 29 top (David Young Wolff).
Bruce Coleman Ltd.: pages 11 top (C.C. Lockwood), 12, 22–23 Dr. Eckart
Pott. Corbis Images: pages 24 (Patrick Ward), 25 top (Tim Page), 28
(Anthony Cooper/Ecoscene).

Artwork: Raymond Turvey.

Note to parents and teachers: Every effort has been made by the publisher to ensure that websites listed are suitable for children, that they are of the highest educational value, and that they contain no inappropriate or offensive material. However, because of the nature of the Internet, it is impossible to guarantee that the contents of these sites will not be altered. We strongly advise that Internet access is supervised by a responsible adult.

CONTENTS

WATER FOR LIFE

We need water to live. Water makes up about two-thirds of our bodies. We can live for weeks without food, but only a few days without water.

Water world

Water covers about two-thirds of the Earth's surface. It is mostly salty water, in seas and oceans. We cannot drink this. Instead we need fresh water, without salt.

Watering a field of crops. All plants need water to grow.

From space, we can see that most of the Earth is covered by water.

Chad, in Africa, is very dry. People must collect water from wells every day.

Farming

In some countries, two-thirds of all the water is used by farmers. They need it for their crops. Their animals need water to drink.

Plenty of water

In richer parts of the word, it is easy for people to get fresh water. It comes into homes through faucets. There is water to drink, and water for washing. People can use this water for their gardens, and even to fill swimming pools.

Not enough water

In poorer counties, many people do not have water in their homes. They have to walk long distances to reach faucets or wells. The amount of fresh water in the world never changes. But there are more people in the world, so we all need to use less water.

WATER CYCLE

People, and the plants and animals that live on land, need fresh, liquid water in order to live. Yet only a tiny amount of water on Earth is fresh water. Most of this is frozen, and is solid ice.

Different forms

Water becomes solid ice when it freezes. This happens at 32°F (0°C). When ice gets warmer, it melts. It becomes liquid water. As liquid water gets warmer, it changes into a gas called water vapor. We say it **evaporates.**

How clouds form

Water vapor rises into the sky. It cools, and turns into millions of tiny droplets of water. We say the water vapor has **condensed.** Millions of water droplets form rain clouds. The droplets join, and form raindrops.

The North and South Poles are covered with frozen, fresh water.

An endless cycle

Raindrops fall to the ground. Water flows into rivers, lakes, and the sea. This water evaporates again. This endless process is the water cycle.

Water evaporates from the leaves of this forest. The water vapor condenses to become clouds.

The water vapor forms clouds and rain. Rain falls back to the ground. It forms streams.

THE WATER CYCLE
The arrows show the water as it moves into the sky and back to the ground.

Water vapor blows inland from the sea.

Water evaporates from land.

Seawater evaporates. Water vapor rises into the sky. Salt is left behind.

Rain falls back into the sea.

Rivers and streams empty fresh water into the sea.

USING SALTWATER

The water in the sea is salty. You can taste the salt if you swim in the sea, and then lick your lips. Fresh water is found in rivers and lakes.

Try this

Put a saucer of salty water in a sunny place. After a while, the water evaporates. It leaves the salt behind on the saucer.

Salt in water

There are about 1.2oz (35g) of salt in $^1/_4$ gallon (1 liter) of seawater. Mostly, it is the kind of salt used in cooking.

These people in Sri Lanka are collecting salt from seawater. They trap the water, and let it evaporate. The salt is left behind.

Life at sea

Many plants and animals live in or near fresh water. The salt in seawater would kill them. But there are plants and animals that can live in salty seawater. We say they are adapted to do this.

Green turtles are adapted to live in salty water.

Making fresh water

In some parts of the world, people get fresh water from seawater. They boil the seawater, so the water evaporates. The salt is left behind. They collect the water vapor and cool it. This makes it condense, or turn to liquid. Making fresh water this way is called **desalination**.

Eco Thought

Desalination is expensive. In the Middle East, there are rich countries, where people can afford to make fresh water from the sea. In many poor countries, there is too little fresh water. But people cannot afford desalination.

In Gibraltar, these concrete slopes are used to collect fresh rainwater.

DAMS AND LAKES

Most fresh water we use comes from lakes and rivers. Sometimes, we make lakes specially to store fresh water.

A new water system brings fresh water to a village in Cambodia, in Asia.

Building reserves

We can make a lake by building a dam across a river. A dam is a wall that holds back river water. A lake, called a **reservoir,** forms behind the dam. Pipes carry the water from the reservoir to cities, towns, and farms, where people can use it.

On the Ground

Around the world, dams make new water systems. These systems bring water to many millions of people who live in dry areas where not much rain falls.

Power from water

We can use dams to make electricity. As water moves in a dam, it turns a wheel called a **turbine**. This drives a machine called a generator, which changes movement into electricity. It does not produce any harmful substances, such as smoke in the air. But dams and reservoirs can make big changes to the environment. If there is less water in rivers because of the dams, the numbers of plants and animals that live in them changes, too.

This dam in the USA provides electricity for nearby towns.

On the Ground

When a river floods, it spreads mud over the land. This helps to make the soil **fertile**, so crops grow well. A dam stops this, and the soil becomes less fertile.

This is a power plant in India. Water from the Krishna River is used to make electricity.

11

UNDERWATER STORE

When it rains, water seeps into the ground. It travels down, until it reaches rocks that it cannot flow through. We say these rocks are impervious. The ground above these rocks fills with water.

A store of water

Ground filled with water is called an **aquifer.** The top of the aquifer is called the **water table.** In wet weather, the water table is closer to the surface. In dry weather, it is farther down. We can reach the water table by digging a well.

Springs

A spring happens when the water table bubbles up to the surface. In a desert, the water may collect to form an **oasis.**

This oasis is in the desert in Peru, South America. It provides water for the town of Huacachina.

Eco Thought

Once, there was a water table near the surface in Mexico City. But, now, so much water has been used that wells must be almost 2 miles (3km) deep.

Women in Malawi, in Africa, collect water from an artesian well.

Deep water

Some aquifers are very deep. Water is trapped between layers of rock, and the heavy ground above presses down on it. When people dig a well, this pressure is released. It forces water to the surface. This is an artesian well.

Eco Thought

There is water in aquifers under the Sahara Desert. Some of this has been there for thousands of years.

HOW A SPRING FORMS

A WELL AND AN ARTESIAN WELL

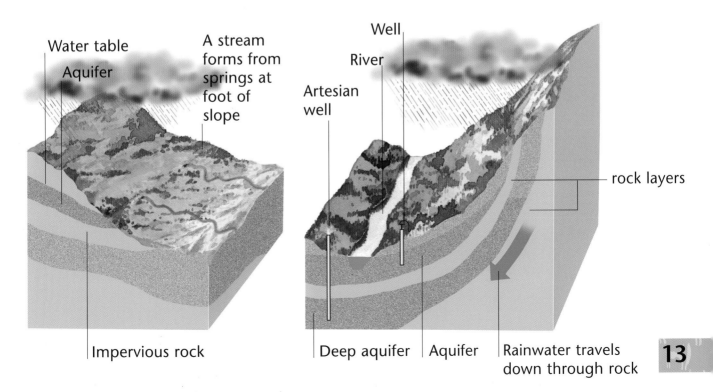

Water table
Aquifer
A stream forms from springs at foot of slope
Impervious rock

Well
River
Artesian well
rock layers
Deep aquifer | Aquifer | Rainwater travels down through rock

CLEAN WATER

We need clean water to drink. Water in wells is usually clean. This is because the ground filters out dirt.

Dirty water

The water in lakes, reservoirs, and rivers may contain germs, which can cause disease. It may also contain sand, mud, rotting leaves, and even dead animals. It has to be cleaned before it is safe for us to drink it.

Reservoir water needs cleaning before it is sent to our homes.

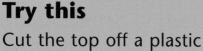

Try this

Cut the top off a plastic bottle. Make some holes in the bottom. Fill the bottle with sand, and pour soapy water through it. The sand will filter out a lot of the soap.

Water for drinking

A **treatment plant** is a place where water is made clean and safe. The water goes into special tanks, where large bits of dirt sink to the bottom. It goes through a filter, to get rid of more dirt. Finally, chlorine gas is added, to kill any germs.

In the United Kingdom, a lot of clean water is wasted. It leaks from old pipes like these.

Safe to drink

In many parts of the world, there are not enough water-treatment plants. People must use dirty water from rivers and lakes. They need to boil this, to kill any germs. It is better to dig deep wells. Well water is usually clean, but digging wells is expensive.

An African girl drinks clean, fresh water from a pipe.

WASTE WATER

The dirty water from baths, toilets, and kitchens is called sewage. It is important to clean sewage before it is safe to put it back into rivers and seas.

Sewage treatment

Sewage is cleaned at a treatment plant. The water goes through screens, to get rid of large objects, such as plastic. Then the water goes to tanks. Here solid waste sinks to the bottom. The water from the tanks is sprayed over stones. These have tiny living things, called **bacteria,** among them. The bacteria help clean the water and make it safe.

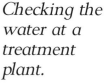

Checking the water at a treatment plant.

Farmers' friend

Solid waste is useful. It can be made into **fertilizer,** for farmers to use on their land.

On the Ground

Plants such as reeds can help clean water. Bacteria live in the reeds. They produce substances that clean the sewage. The water is then safe to go into rivers and streams.

Water is sprayed over stones. Bacteria among the stones help get rid of germs in it.

Carp ponds

In some countries, people pump sewage into ponds. It goes into one pond, then another, and then another. In each pond, bacteria make the water cleaner. People sometimes keep fish called carp in these ponds. The carp eat the sewage, and people eat the carp.

Bacteria live in these ponds among the water plants. They help make sewage safe and clean.

17

POLLUTED WATER

When water contains dangerous dirt and chemicals, we say it is polluted. There are many kinds of pollution. Sewage and the waste from animals' bodies are a kind of pollution. So are fertilizers, and chemicals from factories.

Sewage pours into the sea, before it has been properly cleaned.

When factories make things, they often use huge amounts of water.

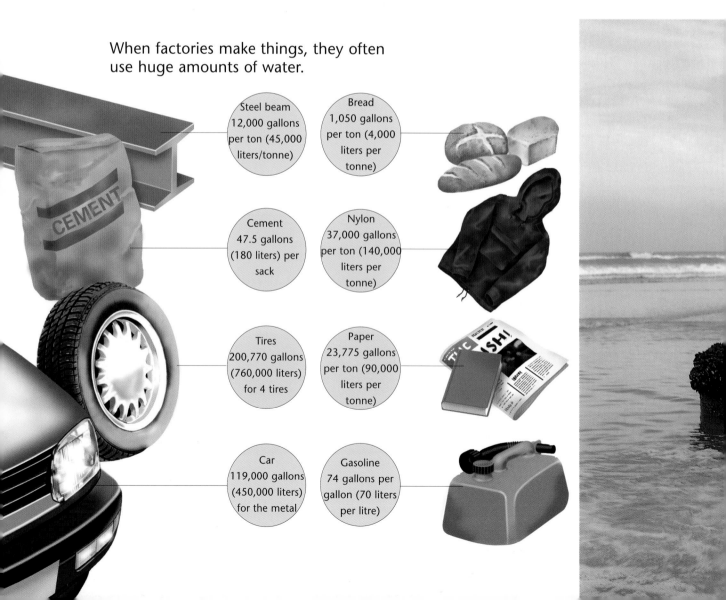

Steel beam
12,000 gallons per ton (45,000 liters/tonne)

Bread
1,050 gallons per ton (4,000 liters per tonne)

Cement
47.5 gallons (180 liters) per sack

Nylon
37,000 gallons per ton (140,000 liters per tonne)

Tires
200,770 gallons (760,000 liters) for 4 tires

Paper
23,775 gallons per ton (90,000 liters per tonne)

Car
119,000 gallons (450,000 liters) for the metal

Gasoline
74 gallons per gallon (70 liters per litre)

Cleaning up

In many countries, people have made laws about keeping water clean. Factories are not allowed to put dirty water into rivers. Sewage has to be cleaned. Rivers that were once dirty are now clean. Fish and other water animals can live in them again.

Polluting the sea

Many harmful substances get into the sea. Factories pour waste into it. People dump garbage into it. This can harm the creatures that live in the sea. Although there are often laws to stop this, not everyone obeys them.

Scientists in the Arctic test water for pollution.

WATER AND FARMS

Plants need water to grow. If there is not enough rain, farmers must water their crops. We call this irrigation.

A boy in Indonesia waters plants.

Channels and sprinklers

Plants need fresh water. Farmers have to find ways of getting this to their crops. In many parts of the world, they dig ditches called **channels** across their fields. They fill these with fresh water to **irrigate** their crops. Today, on modern farms, farmers may use huge machines called sprinklers. These spray water onto the crops.

Eco Thought
Together, all the farm animals in the world use 16 billion gallons (60 billion liters) of water every day.

Trickle and drip

Some farmers use pipes to water their crops. These run under the leaves of the plants. They drip water onto the soil around each plant. This saves water, because shade from the leaves stops the water from evaporating.

*Water flows in **irrigation** channels, so these lettuces can grow.*

This channel of water is for irrigating crops.

Salty soil

Even fresh water has a little salt in it. When land is irrigated, some water evaporates. The salt remains behind. If irrigation is done badly, the soil gets too salty for crops to grow.

21

NO RAIN

In some parts of the world, there is very little rain. Some years, there is no rain at all. We call this a drought.

Drought

When there is a **drought**, crops cannot grow. There is no food or water for animals, and many die. People, too, may die because they do not have enough food. This is a **famine.**

Helping out

In a famine, people become weak and hungry. Organizations called aid agencies may send food, water, and medicines. People need this help until the rains come again.

This aircraft is bringing food to Sudan, in Africa, during a drought.

Deserts are the driest places on Earth. Many animals die of thirst.

Eco Thought

Rain hardly ever falls on the Atacama Desert in South America. There was no rain at all from 1571 to 1971.

People planting trees. The roots will help hold water in the soil.

Better solutions

Scientists have found better ways to grow crops in dry places. For example, they have found that it is good to leave stones in the soil. These make cool, shady places for young plants to grow. Trees shade crops, too, and hold water in the soil.

On the Ground

When rain falls on dry slopes, it may wash soil away. Farmers can stop this happening by cutting flat steps, called terraces, into hillsides.

CHANGING CLIMATE

The climate of the Earth is getting warmer and warmer. This is called global warming.

Greenhouse gases

In a greenhouse, the glass traps the heat of the sun. The greenhouse gets warmer. Some gases in the air trap heat, so the Earth becomes warmer. We call these **greenhouse gases.**

On the Ground

In Bangladesh, in Asia, much of the land is only a few yards (meters) above the level of the sea. If the sea level rises, it will flood this land. Millions of people will lose their homes.

Steam and greenhouses gases are coming out of the chimneys of this power plant.

More storms

Global warming may bring many changes to the world's weather. Some places may get less rain. In other places, there may be more storms, with heavy rain and dangerous floods.

Rising sea

As the water in the sea gets warmer, the ice at the Poles will begin to melt. Sea levels will rise. This will cause floods in low-lying land.

This is a river in Cambodia, after heavy rain. Water is flooding over the land around it.

Planning ahead

Many parts of the world may become drier because of global warming. We must prepare for this. Some countries may need to build more reservoirs, to store more water.

A drought has killed this farmer's crops. Global warming may bring more droughts.

SHORTAGES

When there is not enough water, this is a shortage.

This was once a lake in California. Nearly all the water has been used up by people.

On the Ground

Los Angeles does not have enough water. Extra water comes in pipes, from 105 miles (170km) away.

Lots of people enjoy using swimming pools, but they use up huge amounts of fresh water.

Vacation resorts

Many people take vacations in dry parts of the world. They stay in hotels, which have swimming pools and lots of bathrooms. One bathroom may use more water than local people have all day. Sometimes, water is turned off for part of the day, to stop people from using so much.

Water for wildlife

We can get more water by digging more wells. We can also build more dams, and take more water from rivers. This can make water disappear from other places. Rivers and lakes may dry up. Fish die, and water animals have nowhere to live.

Saving water

We need to find ways of saving water, so that there is enough for everyone. People who live in rich countries use the most water, and also waste a lot of water. It is important to cut back on waste. If we all try to do this, there may be enough water for everyone.

People in richer countries use a lot of fresh water. In poor, dry countries, people use much less.

HOW MUCH WATER
WE USE EACH DAY

USA (in a town):
79 gallons
(300 liters)

Nigeria (in a town):
37 gallons (140 liters)

India (in a village):
8 gallons (30 liters)

Madagascar (in a village): 1.5 gallons (6 liters)

WHAT CAN WE DO?

We can all save water, and not waste it. This is important, even if there seems to be plenty of water where we live.

Helping at home

Be careful when you are brushing your teeth or washing your hands. Don't leave the faucet running. This wastes water. Toilets use a lot of water when we flush them. Water companies can help you find ways to use less water. For example, showers use less water than baths.

Collect rainwater, to use in the garden.

Try this

Put a plug in the bath while you have a shower. See how much water you use. Then have a bath. Which uses more water?

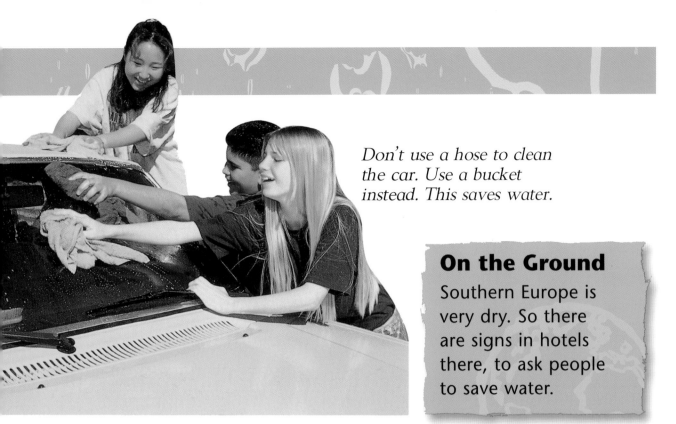

Don't use a hose to clean the car. Use a bucket instead. This saves water.

On the Ground

Southern Europe is very dry. So there are signs in hotels there, to ask people to save water.

Considering others

Poorer countries need to find ways of building good water supplies. Richer countries can send experts and money to help with this. Countries must be careful when they build dams, or take river water. Countries must agree with one another, so everyone gets a fair share of water.

In Burkina Faso, in Africa, people build tanks like this to store water.

FACT FILE

Water wants

Farmers use around 80 percent of all the water in the world. If you put together all the land they irrigate, it would be as big as India.

Melting ice

If all the ice in the world melted, our seas would rise by 197ft (60m).

In space

In 1973, Skylab carried 790 gallons (3,000 liters) of water into space. This lasted three months. The crew had to reuse it more than six times.

Heavy users

Someone in New York City uses about 79 gallons (300 liters) of water each day. A Kenyan only uses just more than 1 gallon (5 liters).

Water within

There are about 9 gallons (35 liters) of water in a teenager's body.

Fatal thirst

Around four million children die each year from drinking dirty water. That adds up to nearly 11,000 children dying every day.

A costly drink

Bottled mineral water is expensive. It costs a thousand times more to produce than faucet water.

Fake lake

The biggest reservoir in the world is Lake Volta, in Ghana. Its shore is 4,500 miles (7,250 km) long.

Population problem

There are 11 million people in Cairo, in Egypt. But the water and sewage system was made long ago, for only two million.

GLOSSARY

Aquifer A layer of rock that stores water. The ground above and below it will not let water pass through it, so it stays in the aquifer.

Bacteria A kind of very tiny living thing, too small to see without a microscope. Some bacteria help break down harmful substances in sewage, and make it safe.

Channel A kind of ditch to carry water.

Condense A change from gas to liquid. For example, when water vapor condenses, it becomes liquid water.

Desalination Taking the salt out of seawater, to make fresh water.

Drought A long time without enough rain.

Evaporate To change from a liquid to a gas. Water in the sea evaporates and becomes water vapor as the Sun heats it.

Famine When there is not enough food. People may starve to death.

Fertile Where crops grow well.

Fertilizer Substances that farmers add to soil to make their crops grow better.

Global warming The way that the Earth is getting warmer.

Greenhouse gas A gas in the air that traps heat. These gases are formed when things are burned. For example, power plants produce greenhouse gases.

Impervious Something that things cannot pass though. Impervious rock is rock that water cannot pass through.

Irrigation Watering crops.

Oasis A place in a desert where water bubbles to the surface and makes a pool of water.

Reservoir An artificial lake that stores a large amount of water. People in cities and towns can use this water. Farmers may need it for irrigation.

Sewage Waste water, such as waste from toilets and dirty water from washing machines.

Treatment plant A place where dirty water is made clean and safe for people to use and to drink.

Turbine A kind of wheel that is used to make electricity. A stream of water turns a turbine, and this energy creates electricity.

Water table The place under the ground where the rocks and soil are filled with water.

INDEX